ALL ABOUT

The Living
WORLD

ALL ABOUT
The Living
WORLD

p

Author
Steve Parker

Designers
Diane Clouting and Phil Kay

Editor
Linda Sonntag

Project Management
Raje Airey and Liz Dalby

Artwork Commissioning
Susanne Grant

Picture Research
Kate Miles and Janice Bracken

Additional editorial help from
Lesley Cartlidge and Libbe Mella

This is a Parragon Book
This edition published in 2000
Parragon, Queen Street House, 4 Queen Street, Bath, BA1 1HE, UK
Copyright © Parragon 1999

Produced by Miles Kelly Publishing Ltd
Bardfield Centre, Great Bardfield, Essex, England CM7 4SL

ISBN 0-75253-602-8

Printed in Italy by G.E.P. Cremona

CONTENTS

The Variety of Living Things   8-9

The Plant Kingdom   10-11

How Plants Work   12-13

Plants and People   14-15

The Animal Kingdom   16-17

From Jellyfish to Starfish   18-19

From Crabs to Cockroaches   20-21

Fishes   22-23

Amphibians   24-25

Reptiles   26-27

Birds   28-29

Mammals 1   30-31

Mammals 2   32-33

Animals and People   34-35

Living World in Peril   36-37

Index   38-39

Acknowledgements   40

THE LIVING WORLD

ALL ABOUT THE LIVING WORLD is divided into fifteen different topics, each covered by a double page spread. On every spread, you can find some or all of the following:

- Main text to introduce the topic

- The main illustration, designed to inform about an important aspect of the topic

- Smaller illustrations with captions, to describe aspects of the topic in detail

- Photographs of unusual or specialized subjects

- Fact boxes and charts, containing interesting nuggets of information

- Projects and activities

THE VARIETY OF LIVING THINGS

THERE ARE MANY different kinds of living things. Look around yourself and you may see grass, trees, flowers and other plants. Also insects, spiders, birds and other animals. (And, of course, people.) But in an unfamiliar place, like a mountain-top or seashore pool, it could be difficult to identify living things, or even tell them apart from non-living ones. A mountain 'pebble' could be a stone-plant. A seashore 'pebble' could be a mussel or oyster. What makes something alive, compared to non-living things like water, diamonds, sand and clouds? Living things have three main features. First, they take in some form of energy and use it for life processes. Second, they take in raw materials and use them to grow. Third, they reproduce or breed – make more of their kind.

The five kingdoms

Many years ago, people thought there were two kingdoms of living things – plants and animals. Fungi such as mushrooms were regarded as strange types of plants. However, most biologists now agree there are five kingdoms – monerans, protists, fungi, plants and animals. Differences between kingdoms include their types of microscopic cells (see Smallest units of life) and how they get their energy. Each moneran or protist is only one cell. Each plant or animal has many cells. Some fungi are one cell, others many. However, there are other schemes for grouping or classifying living things into kingdoms. Some of these schemes are made up of more than 20 kingdoms.

WHO NEEDS TO KNOW?

The study of life and living things is called biology. Why learn about it? There are many reasons:

● To improve farming methods, for more and healthier foods.

● To care properly for our pets, farm animals and other creatures.

● To fight harmful living things, such as germs and parasites, that cause disease.

● To understand about wild plants and creatures, conserve nature, reduce the effects of pollution and improve our environment.

● To understand how our own bodies work, and to improve our health and medical care.

Life all around us

A countryside scene may seem quiet and peaceful. But living things are growing, thriving, feeding and breeding. In this type of landscape, most of the living things are there because people want them. Large animals like cows and horses munch the grass, and the grass itself is grown to feed them. The plants of the hedgerow are trimmed and help to keep these livestock animals in their fields. But more natural or 'wild' living things can still occur. Poppies brighten the roadside verges, and rabbits hide in the long grass. Some people may regard these as pests. However, other people say that pests are simply living things existing where they are not wanted.

Petals of poppy flower

Ripe poppy seed-head

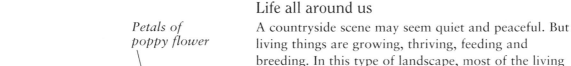

Monerans

The three kinds of
monerans are viruses,
bacteria and blue-green
algae. Their unique
feature is that inside the
cell, the genetic material
(DNA) is not contained
in a bag-like nucleus (see
Smallest units of life).

● Billions of bacteria live
almost everywhere.
Helpful bacteria make
dead things rot away for
natural recycling.
Harmful bacteria cause
diseases such as typhoid.

● Blue-green algae
(cyanobacteria) live
mainly in fresh water and
form 'scum' on ponds.

● Viruses are the tiniest,
simplest life-forms. They
can only live by taking over another cell, destroying it in the
process. They cause many diseases, such as measles, common cold
and influenza (flu).

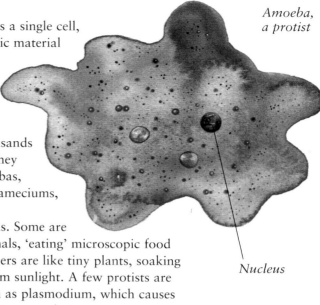

*Viruses can be
dried out as
crystals, yet
still come back
to 'life'*

Protists

Each protist is a single cell,
with its genetic material
inside a bag-
like nucleus.
A drop of
pond water
or sea water
contains thousands
of protists. They
include amoebas,
euglenas, parameciums,
diatoms and
foraminiferans. Some are
like tiny animals, 'eating' microscopic food
particles. Others are like tiny plants, soaking
up energy from sunlight. A few protists are
harmful, such as plasmodium, which causes
the tropical disease malaria.

*Amoeba,
a protist*

Nucleus

Fungi

Mushrooms, toadstools, brackets, moulds, microscopic
single-celled yeasts, rusts and mildews are all fungi. They
make digestive juices which soak into a dying or dead
living thing, and break it into simpler substances. The
fungus then absorbs these simple substances through
its outer covering. Fungi make once-living things
decay and rot away, as part of nature's recycling
processes. Some are harmful, causing diseases such as
athlete's foot. Rusts attack farm crops and dry rot
fungus makes wood weaken and decay, causing great
damage to buildings and timber structures. However,
other fungi are useful – yeasts make bread, beer and wine.

Smallest units of life

All living things are made of microscopic
building blocks or single units called cells.
Inside a cell (except a moneran) is a
control centre, or nucleus. This contains
the genetic material, DNA. The nucleus
floats in jelly-like cytoplasm. The whole
cell has a covering, the cell membrane.
There are many other structures or
organelles inside the cell, mostly made of
folded sheet-like membranes. Most cells
are about one-tenth
to one-
hundredth of a
millimetre
across.

Nucleus

Cytoplasm

Cell membrane

Evolution of life

Life began on Earth more than 3,000 million years
ago, in the seas. The first living things were probably
microscopic jelly-like blobs, similar to monerans today.

Over time, many
kinds of bigger, more
complicated living
things appeared,
thrived, but then died
out. This gradual
change of living
things through time
is called evolution.
The main evidence
for it is fossils –
remains of once-
living things, which
were slowly turned to
stone and preserved
in the rocks.

*Fossil remains of the first
known bird, Archaeopteryx,
from about 150 million
years ago*

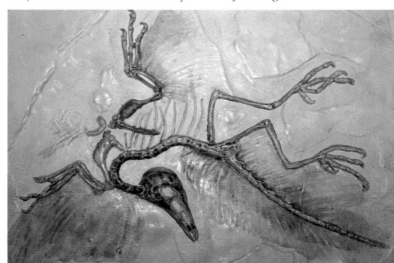

THE PLANT KINGDOM

PLANTS MAKE UP the second biggest kingdom of living things, after animals. They include familiar garden, countryside and farm plants such as grasses, flowers, herbs, bushes and trees. There are also less familiar kinds of plants such as liverworts, mosses, ferns and algae. Many plants grow flowers – but not all. Many have roots in the ground – but not all. The key feature of all plants is that they soak up or trap light energy from the Sun, using it to live and grow. They do this with a green substance known as chlorophyll. So most plants are green, or have green parts, like leaves. However some plants have other coloured substances, so they may be a different colour, like red seaweeds. Plants are grouped according to their bodily features, as shown opposite.

Why plants differ

Each kind of plant has a special shape and features, to survive in its habitat. For example, a desert cactus has spines to stop animals nibbling it, and a stretchy barrel-shaped stem to store precious water. The small grey-brown flower called edelweiss lives on high mountains and has furry leaves to keep out the cold. Most plants take in nutrients from the soil, so they cannot grow where soil lacks nutrients. But the venus flytrap can. Its spiked leaves close quickly around a fly or other insect, like grasping hands, and absorb the nutrient-packed juices from the insect's body.

Seaweeds (algae)

Algae are the simplest plants. They include seaweeds such as wracks, oarweeds and kelps, and some kinds of pond and river waterweeds. They are 'simple' because they do not have many specialized parts, such as roots to take in water. Algae soak up nutrients from the water all around them.

Mosses and liverworts

Mosses have small, low-growing stems with leaf-like parts called scales. Liverworts have flat lobes that look like soft, fleshy leaves. Both lack true roots, to take up water from the soil. So they must soak up moisture from their surroundings, which is why they grow only in damp, shady places.

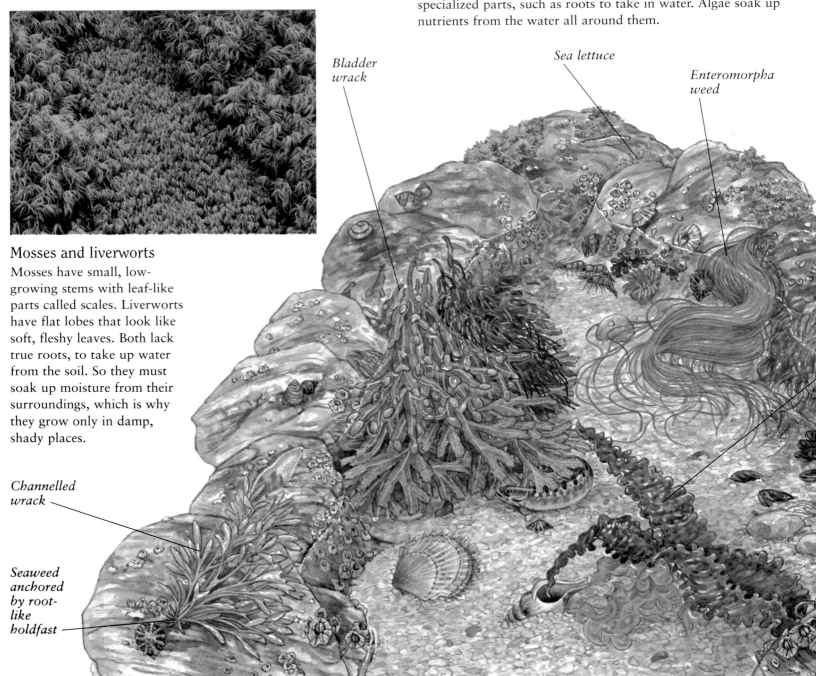

Bladder wrack

Sea lettuce

Enteromorpha weed

Channelled wrack

Seaweed anchored by root-like holdfast

- Fossils show that the first plants appeared on Earth more than 1,000 million years ago. They lived in the sea and probably looked like small lumps of green slime.
- Gradually these earliest plants developed into larger algae, or seaweeds.
- About 400 million years ago, small moss-like plants spread slowly on to the rocky, empty land.
- By 300 million years ago, ferns grew as big as trees, forming steamy, swampy prehistoric forests.
- Some 200 million years ago, forests of conifer trees spread across land, as the first dinosaurs roamed among them.
- Flowering plants appeared about 130 million years ago, bringing bright colours to the landscape.

Ferns and horsetails

A fern has roots anchored in soil, to absorb water and nutrients. It also has specialized tubes inside its body, to carry water and nutrient-rich sap to all its parts. Its leaf-like fronds, held up on a strong, stiff stem, capture sunlight energy. Horsetails are similar but have a stem that looks like a pile of upturned, spiky umbrellas.

Conifers

Conifers are plants with cones – hard, woody parts where the seeds develop. Most conifers grow as bushes or trees, with a strong stem, the trunk. Their leaves are like long, thin needles or hard, rounded scales. Their wood is called softwood. Conifers include pines, firs, spruces and larches. Most conifers shed their leaves slowly and continually and are known as evergreens.

Flowering plants

This is by far the largest plant group, with more than a quarter of a million different kinds, or species. It includes flowers, grasses, rushes, reeds, herbs, the fruits and vegetables we eat, and bushes and trees (apart from conifers). Only flowering plants have true flowers (blooms), which are often very colourful, sweet-smelling and beautiful, as shown on the next page.

Sugar kelp (sea belt)

Orange sea lichen

Lichens

A lichen looks like a small, crusty plant, but it is not a single living thing. It is a combination of a fungus and an algal plant. The fungus part gives strength and support, and the plant part provides food using sunlight. This type of helpful partnership between different living things is called symbiosis. Lichens survive in harsh conditions where plants could not, such as frozen soil or dry rocks. They grow very slowly and are easily damaged by polluted air.

MAIN PLANT GROUPS		
SCIENTIFIC GROUP NAME	ORDINARY NAME	NUMBER OF DIFFERENT KINDS, OR SPECIES
Algae	Seaweeds	6,000
Bryophytes	Mosses	10,000
	Liverworts	14,000
Pteridophytes	Ferns	12,000
	Horsetails	30
	Clubmosses	400
Gymnosperms	Conifers	600
Angiosperms	Flowering plants	250,000-plus

HOW PLANTS WORK

A TYPICAL FLOWERING PLANT has four main body parts. The finger-like roots grow into the soil, anchor the plant firmly and soak up water, minerals and nutrients. The tall, stiff stem holds the leaves and flowers away from the ground, to avoid nibbling animals and dampness. The stem also has tiny pipe-like tubes inside which carry water, minerals and a sweet, sticky fluid called sap, full of minerals and nutrients, around the plant. The leaves soak up energy from sunlight. The flowers make new plants, as shown below.

Food from sunshine

Plants make their food by photosynthesis. This happens mainly in the leaves, which are green because they contain a green substance, chlorophyll. The chlorophyll soaks up or traps energy from sunlight. Meanwhile a gas in air, carbon dioxide, passes through tiny holes, stomata, into the interior of the leaf. And water from the soil soaks through the roots and up the stem, into the leaf. Inside the leaf cells, sunlight energy from chlorophyll joins the carbon dioxide to the water, to make a sweet, energy-rich food called glucose or sugar. This dissolves in the sap and flows to all parts of the plant, providing energy for life.

Leaf cells

Refreshing the air

Photosynthesis produces a gas, oxygen, which passes out of the leaves, into the air. Oxygen is vital because animals, including ourselves, need to breathe it. It helps to break down foods to release the energy in them for life processes. Plants, fungi and other living things also need oxygen, for exactly the same reason. So plant photosynthesis refreshes the air all around the world, replacing the oxygen that all living things use up.

Pollen grains under the microscope

Male parts
Each male cell is in a tiny pollen grain. The grains are inside a bag-like anther, on a tall stalk, the filament. Anther and filament make up the stamen.

Female parts
The female cells, or ovules, are usually inside a fleshy part, the ovary, at the flower's base.

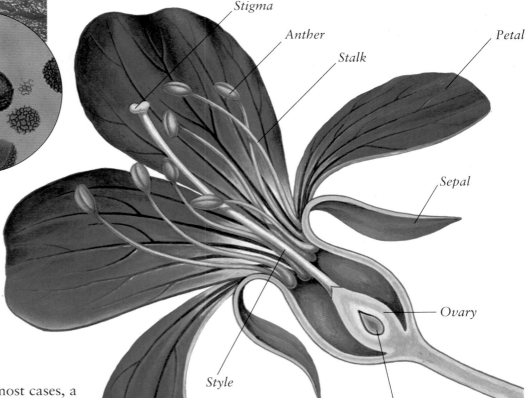

Stigma

Anther

Stalk

Petal

Sepal

Ovary

Style

Ovules

Making new plants

A plant's flowers are for reproduction. In most cases, a flower has male and female parts, called stamens and carpels. The stamen makes tiny powder-like pollen grains, each containing a microscopic male cell. The carpel contains ovules, or female cells. The male cell from one flower reaches the female part of another flower of the same kind, by pollination (see right). When male and female cells join, this is fertilization. The fertilized cell begins to develop into a new plant, inside a hard case, and is known as a seed.

Pollination and fertilization

A pollen grain lands on the carpel's top part, the stigma. A tiny pollen tube grows from the grain, down the carpel's stalk or style, to the ovary. The male cell moves along the pollen tube, down into the ovary. It joins with or fertilizes a female cell, and a new plant begins to develop.

Types of pollination

Pollen grains get from male to female flower parts in various ways. A flower with strong scent, brightly coloured petals and sugary nectar attracts animals such as bees, butterflies, bats and hummingbirds. The animal gets brushed with pollen grains, then carries them to other flowers as it feeds. This is known as animal pollination. In other flowers the pollen grains are so small and light that they blow in the wind. This is wind pollination. Since the flowers of wind-pollinated plants do not need to attract animals, they are usually less colourful and showy. In some water plants, pollen is carried by water currents.

Bee's body gets brushed with pollen grains

Bee collects pollen 'baskets' on legs

Forming seeds

The fertilized egg starts to grow into a tiny new plant, known as an embryo, inside a hard protective case, the seed. For the best chance of growing into a new plant, the seed is carried away from the parent plant, to avoid overcrowding. This is seed dispersal.

Animal-dispersed seeds

In some flowers the seed case becomes thick, soft and tasty – a fleshy fruit. In others it becomes extremely hard and thick – a tough nut. Animals of many kinds eat fruits and nuts. The seeds within often pass through the animal's body undigested. They come out of the other end at a new place, ready to grow.

Windblown seeds

In some flowers, the seeds are small and light, and develop wing-like flaps or sails, or fluffy, parachute-like hairs. These help the wind to blow the seeds to new places. Dandelions and sycamores have these types of wind-dispersed seeds.

Growing seeds

Inside each seed is a young plant, with the beginnings of tiny stem, root and leaves. The seed also contains stored food, in whitish, lumpy parts called cotyledons. The food enables the young plant to germinate – grow out of its case, set down roots, and send its shoot and new leaves up to the Sun.

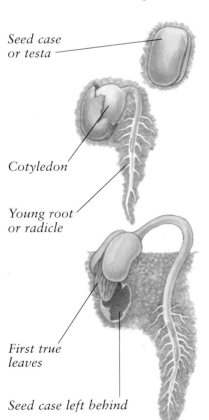

Seed case or testa

Cotyledon

Young root or radicle

First true leaves

Seed case left behind

A typical seed such as a bean has a tough case. It can withstand drying out and lack of water for long periods. But as soon as the seed is exposed to moisture, it begins to develop.

The cells of the baby or embryo plant inside the seed begin to multiply. They begin to use the store of food in the cotyledons. The young root lengthens and grows downwards into the soil.

The root anchors the seed into the soil. The stem begins to straighten. It pulls the shoot and first leaves, sandwiched between the two cotyledons, out of the soil and up into the air.

PRESSING FLOWERS

Identify some colourful common flowers from a garden, using a flower field guide. After getting permission, carefully snip them from their stems and arrange them between two sheets of absorbent paper, such as blotting paper. Put a pile of heavy books on top. Change the absorbent paper each day. After a few days, take out the dried, pressed flowers. You could stick them into a scrapbook and make your own guide book, or use them to decorate pictures or greeting cards.

PLANTS AND PEOPLE

ANIMALS DEPEND ON PLANTS for survival. Many eat leaves, fruits, seeds and other plant parts. Animals also use plants for shelter, such as woodpeckers in tree-trunk holes, and badgers in dens among tree roots. Humans are much the same. We eat plant parts of all kinds, including fleshy fruits such as apples and oranges, nutritious nuts like hazelnuts and peanuts, energy-packed seeds such as wheat (baked into bread) and rice, leaves like lettuce and cabbage, root parts such as potatoes and turnips, herbs and spices like parsley and chilli, even flavourings such as vanilla for ice-cream and cacao for chocolate … The list goes on and is almost endless. Humans also use plants for shelter. Not by living inside trees, but by cutting down trees and using their wood to make houses and other buildings. Timber also makes furniture, cooking utensils, bowls, toys and decorative items like vases and sculptures. Even this book is printed on paper made from trees, which are plants. Trees for the paper, card and board industry are usually conifers or softwoods. They are specially grown in a sustainable way, with new ones planted regularly to replace them.

On the farm

Farm plants include cereals (grasses) such as wheat, barley, rye, rice and millet. There are also fruits such as pears and apples, vegetables like tomatoes and marrows, berries such as blackberries and grapes, tropical mangoes and melons, and all kinds of nuts. To plant experts, all these are fruits, because they contain seeds. They have plentiful energy and nutrients. In the natural world this is to attract animals to eat them, or to help their own seeds grow and germinate. But we grow these plants to eat ourselves or feed to our farm animals.

Combine harvester in wheat field

Plant products

As well as timber, there are innumerable other plant products. The sticky sap from rubber trees makes natural rubber or latex. Fluffy fibres from cotton plants are spun into cotton cloth. Tough fibres of hemp are twisted into ropes. Olives are pressed to yield olive oil for cooking. Can you add to the list?

Cotton harvest

Latex sap drips from cuts in rubber-tree bark into collecting bowl

The many uses of timber
Wood is widely used around the world as a structural material. It is made into huts, sheds, floorboards, bridges, boats, carts, windmills and waterwheels. Bamboo, a very fast-growing grass with a tough, woody stem, makes lightweight scaffolding poles.

Energy from plants
In some places, people cook and heat their homes using fossil fuels such as gas, oil or coal. In other places, the main fuel for cooking and heating is wood. Collecting firewood destroys trees and makes the landscape barren and dusty. However, many people have no alternative for their survival.

Flower ———
Spiny expanded stem ———
Prickly pear (Opuntia)

Plant pests
A weed is a plant growing where we do not want it. Common garden weeds include nettles, bindweed and ragweed. On a larger scale, some plants have been brought to new countries where they have no natural enemies or diseases. So they spread out of control. Prickly pear, a type of cactus, was taken from America to Australia, for use as a spiny hedge-plant. It spread to cover vast areas, driving out local plants and animals. Water hyacinth, originally from tropical America, now chokes lakes and waterways across North America, Africa, Asia and Australia.

Flowers bloom early in artificial daylight and glasshouse warmth

Plant breeding
For centuries, people have chosen or selected plants with features which they wanted, and bred the plants together. This is called selective breeding. The feature may be a special petal colour, bigger fruits, a taller and straighter stem, or resistance to disease. Gradually, the selected plants develop a better version of the feature. The result is thousands of man-made or artificial varieties of plants, in our gardens, parks, farms, fruit orchards, greenhouses, forestry plantations and garden centres.

COMMON BUT RARE
- The African Violet (which is not closely related to the common violets) is one of the world's most common houseplants.
- Over many years it has been bred in a huge range of colours and shapes.
- Yet this plant has all but disappeared from its original wild home, the foothill regions of Tanzania and Kenya in East Africa.
- Collecting plants from the wild threatens many species, especially cacti.

Medicinal plants
Since stone-age times, people have used leaves, sap, berries and other plant parts to ease suffering and heal disease. By trial and error, they found the most helpful kinds. Today, scientists test thousands of plants for medical use. About one-half of modern medicinal drugs are either purified from plants, or based on substances originally extracted from plants. Many more plants wait to be tested in this way – if they are not destroyed first.

Periwinkle *Foxglove* *Opium poppy* *White willow* *Feverfew*

THE ANIMAL KINGDOM

ANIMALS MAKE UP THE BIGGEST kingdom of living
things. They include familiar pets like hamsters and
goldfish, farm animals such as cows and sheep,
and common wild creatures like bugs, slugs, birds,
bats and rats. But the animal kingdom also
includes very strange living things which look more
like space-aliens than Earth creatures. Some live
their entire lives in dark caves, inside rocks or tree-
trunks, or in the ooze on the sea bed. Many
animals can move about actively – but not all.
Barnacles and mussels are stuck to seashore rocks.
Most animals have sense organs such as eyes or
ears – but not all. A sponge cannot see or hear. The
key features of an animal are that its body is made
of many microscopic cells; it eats or consumes
other living things or their parts to obtain energy;
it grows or develops; it can move about at some
stage in its life; and it reproduces to
make more of its kind.

What is this animal?

Is it even an animal? The sea-lily or
crinoid looks more like a flower
growing on the ocean floor. But it is an
upside-down version of the more familiar
starfish. The sea lily waves its feathery
'legs' to gather tiny bits of floating food.
When young and small, it floats and swims in
the ocean, before anchoring to the bottom.

Why animals differ

Each kind of animal has a special body shape and features,
which help it to survive in its habitat. For example, a camel
in the desert has thick fur to protect against hot sun, wide
feet to prevent sinking into soft sand, and a huge stomach to
drink vast amounts of water. Its long eyelashes keep
windblown sand out of its eyes, and its hump contains
stored food in the form of body
fat, which the camel can use
when other food is scarce.
The camel also produces
very dry droppings and
concentrated urine, to
help conserve
precious water.

One-humped or dromedary camel

Grabbing a meal

The gulper eel is a deep-sea fish. It has
an enormous mouth and can eat a
victim bigger than itself. This is useful
because food is very rare in the vast, dark
depths of the oceans. Any victim that comes
near is worth grabbing and eating. The gulper eel's
stomach stretches like a balloon to surround its meal.

ANIMAL EVOLUTION

• Very rare fossils show that the first animals were
probably simple, blob-like jellyfish and worms, in the
sea more than 700 million years ago.

• By 500 million years ago, animals with hard body
cases, such as trilobites and limpet-like shellfish,
inhabited seas and lakes.

• Around 400 million years ago, the first animals
followed early plants on to dry land. These first land-
dwelling creatures were probably millipedes and small
insects.

• By 350 million years ago, amphibians walked on dry
land. Myriad fish, including sharks, swarmed in the
seas.

• The first reptiles evolved by 300 million years ago.

• A great extinction 250 million years ago killed off
many kinds of amphibians and reptiles, and many types
of sea creatures.

• Around 200 million years ago, reptiles called
dinosaurs spread across the land. The first mammals,
small and shrew-like, hid from them.

• Another great extinction 65 million years ago killed
off dinosaurs and many other reptiles, as well as sea
animals such as ammonites.

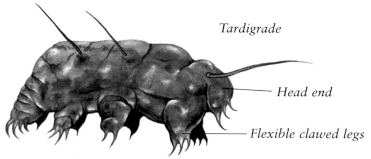

Tardigrade

Head end

Flexible clawed legs

Biggest and smallest

Animals cover a vast range of sizes. The biggest creature ever to live on Earth still swims in the oceans. It is the blue whale, more than 25 metres long and 150 tonnes in weight. Among the smallest animals are water-bears or tardigrades. They resemble short, fat caterpillars with four pairs of flexi-legs, and live mainly in soil or ponds. Some are smaller than the dot on this i.

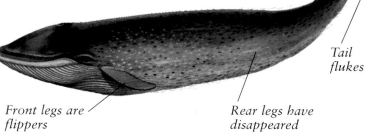

Tail flukes

Front legs are flippers

Rear legs have disappeared

MAIN GROUPS OF ANIMALS

There are probably at least five million different kinds, or species, of animals. They are divided into main groups, or phyla, by their body structure and main features. The biggest group by far is the arthropods. The various groups are described over the following pages.

SCIENTIFIC GROUP NAME	ORDINARY NAME	NUMBER OF DIFFERENT KINDS, OR SPECIES
Poriferans	Sponges	5,000
Cnidarians (Coelenterates)	Jellyfish, anemones, corals	9,500
Platyhelminthes	Flatworms	6,000
Nematodes	Roundworms	12,000
Annelids	Segmented worms such as earthworms	11,500
Arthropods	Insects, spiders, crabs and other crustaceans, centipedes, millipedes	5 million-plus
Molluscs	Shellfish, snails, squid, octopus	80,000
Echinoderms	Starfish, urchins	6,000
Chordates or vertebrates	Fish, amphibians, reptiles, birds, mammals	40,000

Animals from the past

The dinosaurs lived from about 210 to 65 million years ago. Using the remains of their bones, teeth, horns, claws and other hard body parts, preserved as fossils, we can make informed scientific proposals about how they looked and behaved in life. Their droppings also fossilized, showing what they ate. However, the fossils give no clue to the skin colour of dinosaurs. The colours shown in these types of reconstructions are guesswork.

FROM JELLYFISH TO STARFISH

AN INVERTEBRATE IS AN ANIMAL that does not have a backbone or spinal column. More than 30 main groups, or phyla, of invertebrates have soft, jelly-like bodies. The more important and familiar are shown here. They all have a body design which is bilaterally symmetrical – that is, the body has a left and right side. Except for echinoderms, such as starfish. These have a body based on a radial plan, with a centre and parts radiating from it like the spokes of a wheel. (Invertebrates with hard body casings are shown on the next page.)

Starfish and urchins

Members of the large echinoderm group live only in the sea. Their radial or circular body is based on the number five. So most starfish have five arms, or ten, or so on. They move by gliding on hundreds of tiny, sucker-tipped tube-feet on their underside. A sea urchin is like a starfish with its arms curled up and in, and joined together on top to form a ball shape. Like a starfish, an urchin also has a mouth on the underside, which scrapes and rasps food off rocks, and it moves on very long, thin tube-feet. In some kinds of urchins, the protective spines are tipped with poison.

Inside-out stomach

Starfish are deadly predators. They wrap their suckered arms around a shellfish victim and pull hard and long, to prise the shells apart. Then the starfish pours its digestive juices on to the soft flesh inside the shellfish. Finally the starfish turns its own stomach inside out through its mouth and on to the victim, to soak up the soft, soupy meal.

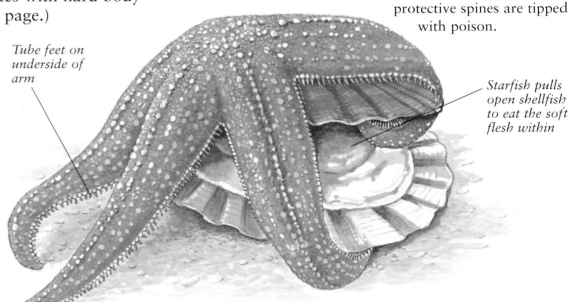

Tube feet on underside of arm

Starfish pulls open shellfish to eat the soft flesh within

Arm tips have simple light-sensitive 'eyes'

Sponges

A sponge has no eyes, ears, brain, mouth, guts or muscles. It is the simplest type of animal – little more than a pile of microscopic cells. It sucks in water though small holes over its body, into a central chamber. Floating particles of food are filtered out using tiny hairs called cilia which line the chamber. The water squirts out through a larger hole, the oscule. Most sponges live in the sea.

Jellyfish, anemones and corals

Anemones have a stalk-like body with a mouth surrounded by waving tentacles. These sting and catch passing animals and pull them down to the mouth. Corals are smaller versions of anemones. Each makes a stony cup around its body, for protection. Over many years, millions of cups build into the rock or a coral reef. A jellyfish has its mouth on the lower side and an umbrella-like body. Nearly all of these animals live in the sea.

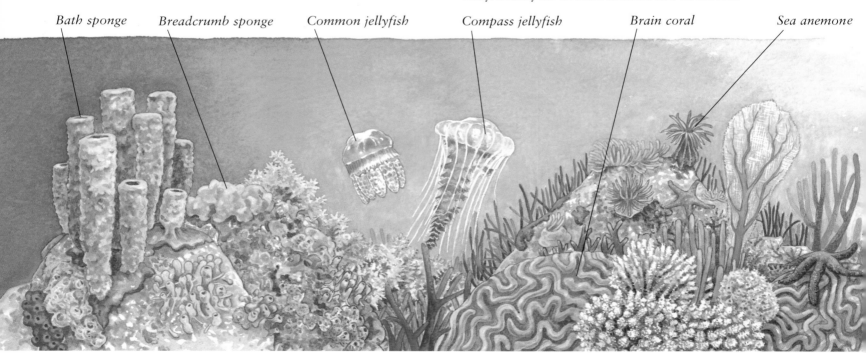

Bath sponge   *Breadcrumb sponge*   *Common jellyfish*   *Compass jellyfish*   *Brain coral*   *Sea anemone*

How invertebrates breed

Most animals breed sexually, when a female and male get together. But some invertebrates can reproduce on their own, asexually. A new, small individual grows from the parent animal, just like a new bud grows from a parent plant. Sponges, corals, jellyfish and flatworms do this. Also, in most animals, an individual is either a female or male. But some invertebrates have both male and female parts in the same body. They are hermaphrodites. They include earthworms, leeches, and various molluscs such as snails. A hermaphrodite rarely mates with itself. It usually teams up with a partner and both produce eggs or babies.

Both fathers and mothers

Snails are hermaphrodites. Each has male and female parts. Two snails mate by twining and writhing together in a bath of frothy, sticky, slimy mucus. Each one passes its male cells, or sperm, to the other, to fertilize its eggs. Then each one lays its eggs.

Flatworms

These are mostly small, soft, flattened, leaf- or ribbon-shaped animals. They have simple eyes to detect patches of light and dark. Some dwell in water. Others slide through leaves in tropical rainforests. Still others are parasites, living on or in other animals, including humans, taking nourishment and shelter from them. The parasites include liver flukes and tapeworms.

Roundworms

A handful of soil teems with tiny roundworms, or nematode worms. The mouth at one end eats food, and wastes pass out of the anus at the other end. Unlike true worms, the body of a nematode is not divided into many similar sections, or segments. Many nematodes are parasites, causing diseases such as hookworm and river blindness.

Other invertebrates

The smaller groups or 'minor phyla' of invertebrates are mainly obscure worm-like creatures that live in out-of-the-way places. For example, horsehair worms in the phylum Nematomorpha number only 80 species, compared to 11,500 species of true worms. Horsehair worms are very long and thin, like the strands of a horse's mane or tail. They live in ponds, lakes, canals and other bodies of still, fresh water – including horse troughs. This gave rise to the legend that they are horse hairs come to life. When young, these worms are parasites of small animals such as insects. The adults coil around water plants.

WATCH WORMS AT WORK

Earthworms are 'nature's gardeners'. They eat and recycle nutrients in dead bits of animals and plants, and their tunnels keep soil well drained. In a large see-through container, such as a big jar or old aquarium, put alternate layers of sand and garden soil. Carefully add a few earthworms from the garden, and put old leaves and twigs on top. Sprinkle on water to keep the wormery damp. After a few days, see how the worms mix up the layers and recycle the leaves.

True worms

Annelid or true worms have a body divided into many similar sections or segments, one behind the other. There are more than 3,000 kinds of earthworms, also lugworms and ragworms on the seashore, and fanworms with their crown of feathery feeding tentacles in shallow water. Leeches, which live mainly in lakes and swamps, have a sucker at each end of the body and feed by sucking blood or body fluids.

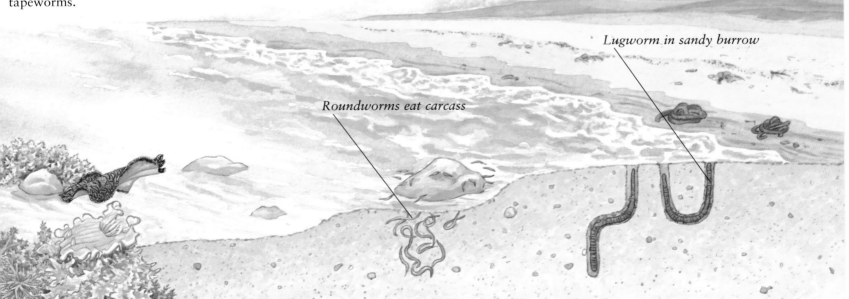

Lugworm in sandy burrow

Roundworms eat carcass

FROM CRABS TO COCKROACHES

OF ALL THE ANIMAL SPECIES in the world, at least nine out of every ten are insects. The insects belong to the major animal group or phylum called the arthropods, a name which means 'joint-legged'. This is because a typical arthropod has a hard, tough body casing, known as an exoskeleton, with flexible joints in the limbs (like our own knees and ankles). These joints allow the creature to walk, run, swim or burrow. Other arthropod groups include the centipedes (chilopods), millipedes (diplopods), crabs and other crustaceans, and spiders and other arachnids.

Inside an insect

Like all arthropods, an insect such as an ant has a strong, rigid outer body casing, the exoskeleton. The insect's body has three main sections. The front, or head, bears two eyes, two antennae or feelers, and mouthparts. The middle, or thorax, has six legs and (in most insects) two pairs of wings. The rear, or abdomen, contains mainly the guts and reproductive parts. The total number of insect species is estimated at more than 5 million.

Antenna

Brain

Heart

Mid gut

Main blood vessel

Malpighian tubes (excretion)

Mouthparts

Main nerve cord

Salivary glands

Hind gut

Acid-making gland

MAIN GROUPS OF INSECTS

There are more than 30 groups (orders) of insects. Biggest by far is the beetles and weevils, with at least half a million species.

SCIENTIFIC GROUP NAME	ORDINARY NAMES
Apterygota	Silverfish, firebrats, springtails and other wingless insects
Orthoptera	Grasshoppers, crickets, katydids
Odonata	Dragonflies, damselflies
Ephemeroptera	Mayflies
Blattodea	Cockroaches
Isoptera	Termites
Mantodea	Mantids such as praying mantis
Dermaptera	Earwigs
Plecoptera	Stoneflies
Phasmida	Stick-insects, leaf-insects
Thysanoptera	Thrips, thunderbugs
Psocoptera	Book-lice
Phthiraptera	Bird-lice, other parasitic lice
Hemiptera	Bugs such as shieldbugs, pondskaters, cicadas, hoppers, aphids, scalebugs
Neuroptera	Lacewings, ant-lions
Coleoptera	Beetles, weevils
Siphonaptera	Fleas
Hymenoptera	Bees, wasps, ants, sawflies
Diptera	True flies such as housefly, gnat, midge, mosquito, cranefly (two wings only)
Lepidoptera	Butterflies and moths

Crabs and other crustaceans

Crustaceans live mainly in the seas and include crabs, lobsters, shrimps, prawns and barnacles. Pond water-fleas, freshwater crayfish and woodlice (sowbugs) are also in this group. So are copepods, which look like pond water-fleas. Copepods live in vast ocean swarms and are among the most numerous animals on Earth. Most crustaceans have two pairs of antennae (feelers), a hard-cased body divided into similar sections or segments, and at least ten pairs of jointed limbs. The total number of crustacean species is about 40,000.

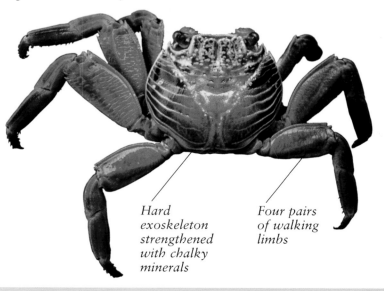

Hard exoskeleton strengthened with chalky minerals

Four pairs of walking limbs

Millipedes

The name means 'thousand-legged', but most millipedes have a couple of hundred legs. There are two pairs on each body segment (unlike centipedes). Millipedes are slow, secretive creatures who prefer the dark and damp, living in forest soil or under bark, eating decaying plant matter. The total number of millipede species is about 8,000.

INSECT RECORDS

● The longest insects are giant tropical stick-insects. Some are more than 30 centimetres in length.

● The heaviest insects are large tropical beetles such as the goliath beetle and rhinoceros beetle. They weigh more than 100 grams.

● The smallest insects are fairy-flies and hairy-winged beetles. They are smaller than the dot on this i.

● The longest-lived insects are probably beetles. Some have been known to live for more than 40 years.

● The most numerous insects are tiny springtails (collembolans) in the soil. They have no wings and cannot fly. But they can jump using a hinged, rod-like part at the end of the body. In a handful of soil there may be many hundreds of springtails.

Centipedes

The name means 'hundred-legged', but most centipede species have fewer than 70 legs. There is one pair per body segment (unlike millipedes). Centipedes are fast, active creatures that prey on worms, insects and other smaller creatures, and kill them with a bite from poison fangs. The total number of centipede species is about 3,000.

Molluscs

On land, familiar molluscs include snails and slugs. But most molluscs live in the sea, such as octopus, squid, cuttlefish, sea-slugs or nudibranchs, and sea-snails like winkles and whelks. Some molluscs have a two-part shell, such as mussels, oysters, clams and scallops. Key molluscan features are a soft, bendy body enclosed in a fleshy 'hood', the mantle. In many molluscs, like snails, the mantle makes a hard protective shell. The total number of mollusc species is about 80,000.

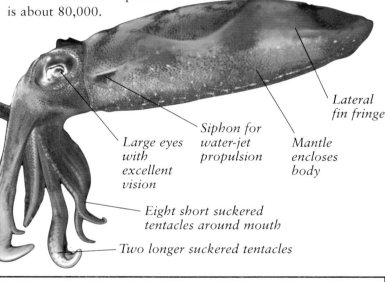

Lateral fin fringe

Large eyes with excellent vision

Siphon for water-jet propulsion

Mantle encloses body

Eight short suckered tentacles around mouth

Two longer suckered tentacles

The cuttlefish, a predatory mollusc

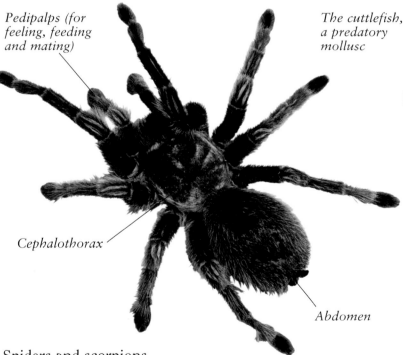

Pedipalps (for feeling, feeding and mating)

Cephalothorax

Abdomen

Spiders and scorpions

Arachnids have four pairs of limbs and a two-part body, the front cephalothorax and the rear abdomen. All spiders catch prey. Many spin silk-strand webs to snare victims and all have a poisonous bite, although less than 50 kinds are dangerous to humans. A scorpion's front pair of legs are large, strong pincers, and its arched tail is tipped with a venomous sting. Tiny mites and ticks are also arachnids. Some of these are parasites and suck blood. The total number of arachnid species is about 70,000.

A SHELL COLLECTION

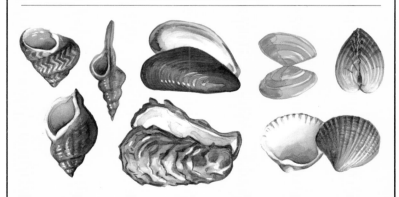

At the seaside, collect a few empty seashells. Wash them in soapy water and let them dry. Identify them using a guide-book and arrange them in a box or on a card sheet. Look at them closely. Are the two parts of an oyster, clam or mussel shell exactly the same? Study their growth rings (as in tree trunks), usually two each year. In sea-snails like whelks, does the shell always twist the same way in different individuals?

FISHES

MANY ANIMALS HAVE 'FISH' as part of their name, such as jellyfish, starfish and crayfish. But these are not proper fishes. A true fish is a vertebrate – an animal with a backbone or spinal column along the middle of its body. A typical fish also lives in water, has a scaly body, breathes using gills on either side of its head, and has broad, flat fins and a tail for swimming. There are more than 21,000 different kinds, or species, of fish. They form the largest group of vertebrates, Pisces. This is bigger than all the other groups of vertebrates (amphibians, reptiles, birds and mammals) added together. They vary in size from the enormous whale shark, more than 13 m long and perhaps 10 tonnes in weight, to the Philippine dwarf goby which is hardly as big as this word.

Parts of a fish

A fish's body is covered with hard scales, which overlap like tiles on a roof, and are transparent to show the skin colour beneath. Many fish have large eyes to see through gloomy water, and nostrils to pick up floating scents and odours. Along either side of the body is a faint line, the lateral line, which senses currents and swirls in the water. This allows the fish to detect other animals moving nearby. Another sense is tiny electricity-detecting pits over the snout and head, especially in many sharks. These pick up tiny electrical pulses made by active muscles of other creatures.

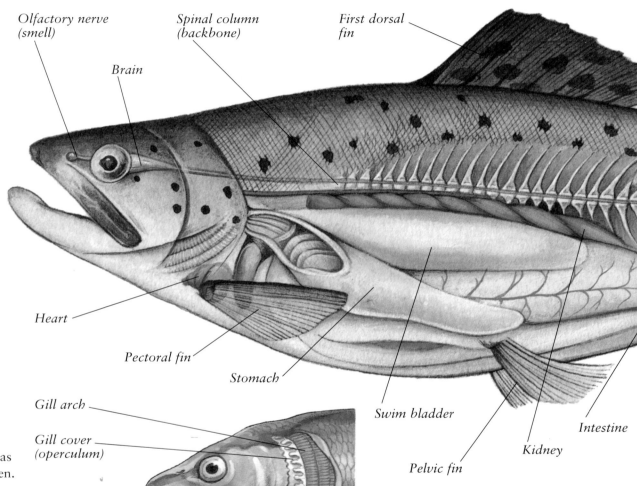

Olfactory nerve (smell)

Spinal column (backbone)

First dorsal fin

Brain

Heart

Pectoral fin

Stomach

Swim bladder

Intestine

Kidney

Pelvic fin

Fish gills and breathing

A fish's gills do the same job as our own lungs – obtain oxygen. The gills are on each side of a fish's head, protected by a bony flap, the gill cover or operculum, with a narrow opening at the rear, the gill slit. Most fish have four gills on each side of the head, although sharks usually have five. Each gill is an arched, delicate, frilly structure with blood flowing through it. Water flows into the fish's mouth, over the gills and out through the gill slit. Oxygen dissolved in the water passes through the thin covering of the gills, into the blood, and is carried around the body. At the same time, the body waste called carbon dioxide passes from the gills into the water, for removal.

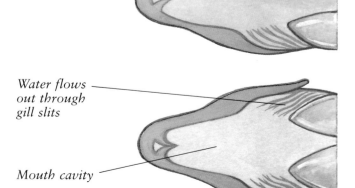

Gill arch

Gill cover (operculum)

Gills slit

Water flows in through mouth

Water flows out through gill slits

Mouth cavity

Fish fins

The fish uses its tail fin to go forwards, and its body fins to steer, turn and stop. Fins vary in shape according to lifestyle. Fast ocean fish have fairly narrow, stiff fins and a crescent- or moon-shaped tail. Slow reef fish have wider, more flexible fins, for close control when darting among rocks. Some can even 'row' with their pectoral fins, without using their tail at all. The area, shape and angle of an individual fin is changed by moving the bony rod-like spines, the fin rays, which support it. Muscles in the fish's body at the base of the fin do this. The first fish appeared on Earth some 500 million years ago. As evolution continued, the fins of some fish became legs and these fish developed into amphibians.

Fish without bones

All fish have an inner skeleton with a skull, ribs and similar parts. But in some fish, this is not made of bone. It is cartilage, or gristle, which is slightly softer and bendier than bone. There are about 710 kinds of cartilaginous fish. They include all sharks, from fast, fierce hunters like the great white, to the small and harmless dogfish. cartilaginous fish also include rays such as the manta and stingray, and skates.

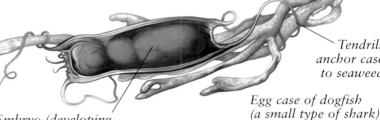

Ray's wing-like sides flap to 'fly' through the water

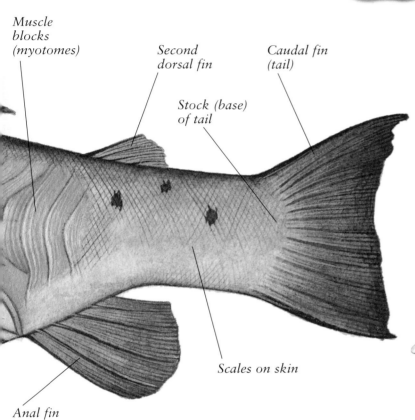

Muscle blocks (myotomes)

Second dorsal fin

Caudal fin (tail)

Stock (base) of tail

Scales on skin

Anal fin

How fish breed

Most fish breed, or spawn, at a certain season. The female lays many eggs, or roe, numbering millions in fish such as cod. She may cast them into the water or hide them in a sheltered place, such as under a rock or among seaweed. The male sheds his sperm, or milt, over the eggs to fertilize them. The eggs then develop and hatch into baby fish, or fry. Only a few fish care for their babies. In the cichlid mouth-brooder, the babies dash inside their mother's mouth when danger threatens.

Tendrils anchor case to seaweed

Embryo (developing baby) in case

Egg case of dogfish (a small type of shark)

In the gloom of deep water, many fish are black, for camouflage in the darkness.

Linophyrne anglerfish

Most ocean fish are streamlined, and silvery or blue-green in colour, for speed and camouflage in the open sea.

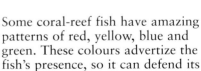

Atlantic cod

Eels are long, thin, snake-shaped fish that hide in small cracks or burrow in mud and sand.

Common eel

Some coral-reef fish have amazing patterns of red, yellow, blue and green. These colours advertize the fish's presence, so it can defend its territory or attract a mate.

Clown fish

Flatfish are flattened from side to side and lie on one side on the sea bed.

Plaice (or flounder?)

Sharks' teeth grow in double or triple rows. When the teeth are worn out, new ones grow to replace them.

Great white shark

AMPHIBIANS

THE AMPHIBIAN GROUP includes about 4,000 kinds, or species, of frogs, toads, salamanders and newts. The name amphibian means 'two lives', because most amphibians have two-part lives. After they hatch from eggs, they live in water, breathe by gills, swim with a tail, and eat plants such as pondweeds. They are called tadpoles. As they grow up, their bodies change shape, growing limbs and losing the tail. This drastic change in body shape is called metamorphosis. (It happens in other groups of animals too, such as most insects.) Then the growing amphibians leave the water to begin the second, adult, part of their lives. They dwell on land, breathe with lungs, walk or hop on their legs, and eat meat in the form of small creatures such as bugs, slugs and worms. However, they have not left the water for ever. At breeding time, they return to water to lay their eggs, so their offspring can grow up in the same way.

Features of amphibians

Most amphibians have the bony inner skeleton and four legs of a typical vertebrate. In frogs and toads, the toes are partly or fully webbed, for effective swimming. Newts have a long tail for the same purpose. Amphibian skin is thin, flexible and moist in most species. It dries out easily, which could result in death, so most amphibians prefer cool, shady, damp places. The skin also produces slimy, foul-tasting substances to deter predators. In some types, such as arrow-poison frogs, even a small smear of these substances can be deadly poisonous. However, some toads have dry skin and because of this they can survive lack of water for a time.

All adult amphibians catch live prey, usually by spotting it with their large eyes, and then gulping it into the wide mouth. The frog has a long, sticky-tipped tongue which it can flick out to grab a small victim like a fly. Large toads can eat prey as big as rats and lizards. Newts are also fierce predators. They tackle small prey such as worms, tiny fish and young tadpoles – even those of their own species.

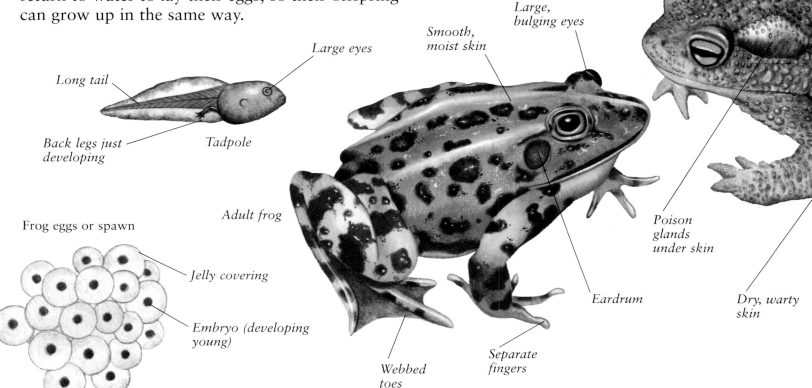

Large eyes

Long tail

Back legs just developing

Tadpole

Smooth, moist skin

Large, bulging eyes

Adult frog

Frog eggs or spawn

Jelly covering

Embryo (developing young)

Poison glands under skin

Eardrum

Dry, warty skin

Webbed toes

Separate fingers

Egg to tadpole to frog

Most adult amphibians return to ponds and pools for the breeding season. In some kinds, males croak or squeak to attract females. A male and female pair up, and the female lays jelly-covered eggs, spawn. The male fertilizes these by adding his milky sperm to them. The jelly coverings of the eggs swell up as they absorb water. The dark, dot-like eggs inside gradually develop and hatch into tiny, feathery-gilled tadpoles, which nibble at pondweed. As the tadpoles grow, the gills shrink and the lungs develop, so the tadpole surfaces to breathe air. The back legs emerge, then the front ones, and the tadpole begins to hunt tiny water creatures. Finally the tail shrinks away and the young adults, or froglets, hop on to land. In the European frog this whole process takes about three to four months, depending on the seasonal temperatures.

Frog or toad?

Most frogs have smooth skin, slim bodies, and move by leaping or jumping. Most toads have lumpy or warty skin, tubby bodies, and move by walking or waddling slowly. In fact there is no single scientific difference between frogs and toads. They all belong to one amphibian sub-group, anurans ('tail-less'). The popular view of the difference between a frog and a toad comes from the common European frog and toad. In other parts of the world, there are toads with smooth, moist skin and frogs with dry skin that tend to waddle. The rear legs of a frog are much longer and stronger than the front legs, for powerful jumping. The front legs soften the landing as the frog finishes its leap. Some sharp-nosed frogs can cover more than three metres in one jump. Salamanders and newts belong to another sub-group of amphibians, the urodelans ('tailed').

Watery home

In temperate regions, most amphibians breed in early spring. By late spring the adults have returned to damp places on land. In tropical rainforests there is moisture everywhere. So many amphibians simply lay their eggs under logs or stones, or under large leaves.

The Pacific giant salamander lives along the Pacific coast of North America

Giant amphibians

The largest amphibians are giant salamanders. The hellbender of eastern North America lives in streams, hunts other water animals and reaches 75 centimetres in length. Asian giant salamanders of Japan and China grow even bigger, more than one metre long.

Legless amphibians

Besides frogs and toads (anurans), and newts and salamanders (urodelans), the amphibian group also includes about 150 species of caecilians, or apodans. These curious creatures look like large earthworms. Most live in forests in warm places, burrowing in the soil. They are active, fierce predators of small soil animals.

Most caecilians are blind and live in burrows underground.

Adult toad

Less webbing on toes

FROM DESERT TO DEEP CAVE

The great majority of amphibians live in warm, moist places such as tropical rainforests. But some dwell in very different habitats.

● The water-holding frog of Australian deserts stays deep under ground until rains come. Then it digs to the surface, feeds and breeds in temporary pools. As the desert dries again, it burrows back under ground.

● The olm is a rare, white, almost blind salamander that lives in total darkness, in rivers and lakes deep in the caves of southern Europe.

● Tree-frogs have wide, sticky pads on their fingers and toes. These grip slippery leaves in their damp tropical forest homes.

● The spotted mole-salamander of North America burrows in the forest floor and eats earthworms, slugs and other soil animals.

The 'water monster'

The axolotl is a rare amphibian of high-altitude freshwater lakes in Mexico. It grows to about 30 centimetres in length and, like other salamanders, it eats smaller animals. Its name means 'water monster' in the Aztec language. The axolotl is like an amphibian that never grows up. Even when adult and able to breed, it still has feathery gills, like a tadpole.

Large gills

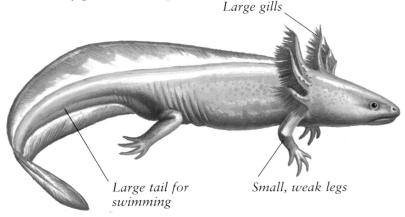

Large tail for swimming

Small, weak legs

HOW TO KEEP TADPOLES

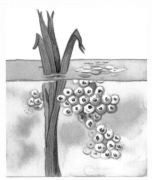

If frogs and toads are common in your area, try keeping some tadpoles for a time, to see how they change their body shape. At the start of the breeding season, ask a knowledgeable adult to collect a fist-sized lump of the spawn. Gather some pond weed from the same place, too. Keep them in an aquarium or similar container, in a cool place away from direct sunlight. Change half of the water every day or two, replacing it with water from the original pond. (Always wear rubber gloves and take great care when handling pond water and wildlife.) Each day, observe the spawn. See how the dark dots grow larger, and then wriggle free of the jelly and emerge as tadpoles. Remove the jelly when this has happened. Keep a diary of when the tadpoles develop their back and front legs. Feed them tiny pieces of dog or cat food. Make sure they have a log or stone to rest on, out of the water, as they begin to breathe air. Finally release them carefully into the wild.

REPTILES

CROCODILES, ALLIGATORS, TURTLES, tortoises, snakes, lizards – all are reptiles. A reptile is a vertebrate animal with a scale-covered body, which lays tough, leathery-shelled eggs. (These do not dry out on land, unlike jelly-covered amphibian eggs.) Most reptiles have four legs, except for two kinds. These are the snakes, and the snake-like reptiles called worm-lizards that burrow in the soil of warm regions. There are about 6,550 kinds, or species, of reptiles alive today. They dwell in most habitats, from lizards in rocky mountains, to turtles and sea-snakes in the middle of the ocean. Many more kinds of reptiles lived in prehistoric times – including the dinosaurs, as shown on earlier pages. It is believed that the first small, shrew-like mammals evolved from reptiles, over 200 million years ago. The first birds probably evolved from reptiles too, more than 150 million years ago. The largest animals ever to walk on Earth were reptiles – giant sauropod dinosaurs from Jurassic times, which weighed over 50 tonnes.

The reptile body

A lizard such as an iguana shows key reptile features. It has an inner skeleton with a backbone, four limbs, a tail, and skin covered with hard, horny scales. The scales do not lie on top of the skin, as in fish. They are embedded in the skin. Most reptiles have big eyes and keen eyesight, ear openings just behind the eyes, nostrils to detect scents in the air (and in water), and a large tongue for tasting food. In some lizards the tongue is very long and can be flicked out to grab small prey.

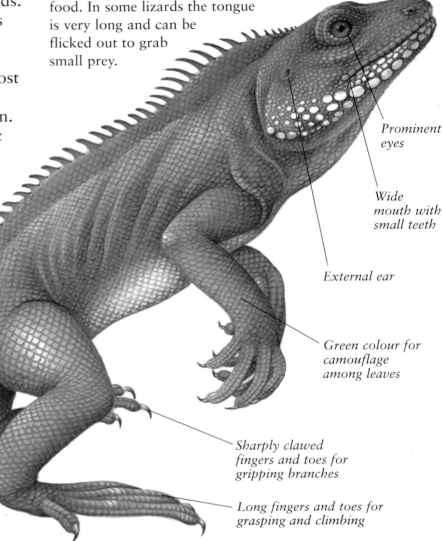

Prominent eyes

Wide mouth with small teeth

External ear

Green colour for camouflage among leaves

Sharply clawed fingers and toes for gripping branches

Long fingers and toes for grasping and climbing

Dry, scaly skin

WHAT DO REPTILES EAT?

Most reptiles eat other animals, either hunting them or scavenging on their dead bodies.

● Many lizards are quick, darting hunters and pursue insects, worms, small birds and mammals such as mice.

● Snakes catch living prey, usually by quiet stealth. They cannot chew and must swallow their victims whole.

● Some turtles lie in wait on the river bed, ready to seize passing fish. Others eat a mixed diet of small animals, carrion, leaves and fruits.

● Sea turtles like the leatherback consume jellyfish, crabs, mussels and other shellfish, crushing them with their strong beak-like jaws.

● Crocodiles and alligators lie low in a river or lake, looking like old logs, and ambush animals who come to drink.

● Very few reptiles eat only plants. One is the marine iguana, a large lizard of the Galapagos Islands in the Pacific, which dives into the sea to chomp on seaweeds.

Turtles

Turtles and terrapins in water, and land-dwelling tortoises, have a body encased in a large, strong, domed shell. The upper part of the dome is the carapace, and the lower part is the plastron. The animal draws its head, legs and tail into the shell for protection. These reptiles are among the longest-lived of all creatures. Spur-thighed tortoises in Europe, eastern box turtles in North America, and giant tortoises on Pacific islands have survived to great ages, some for more than 100 years.

Green turtle

Crocodiles

The largest reptile is the estuarine or salt-water crocodile of the Indian and Pacific Oceans, more than 7 metres long. A croc swims by swishing its tall, flattened tail, and can run surprisingly fast on land. Caimans are crocodilians from swampy areas of Central and South America.

TYPES OF REPTILE		
SUB-GROUP	SCIENTIFIC NAME	NUMBER OF SPECIES
Lizards	Lacertilians	3,750
Snakes	Serpentes	2,400
Turtles, tortoises and terrapins	Chelonians	240
Crocodiles, alligators and caimans	Crocodilians	22
Tuatara	Rhynchocephalians	1
Worm-lizards	Amphisbaenids	140

The Nile crocodile grows to about 6 metres in length.

Sand viper

Deadly snakes

Snakes are reptiles without legs. They move by wriggling and writhing and pushing against tiny bumps in the ground. Some types, like boas, tilt the scales on the lower body for grip. Most snakes creep near a victim and strike with their sharp fangs. Pythons and boas coil around the victim and squeeze or constrict it to death. About 400 of the 2,400 kinds of snakes are poisonous, jabbing venom into the victim with sharp teeth. Feared venomous snakes include cobras, mambas, kraits and tiger snakes, and members of the viper family such as the bushmaster, cottonmouth, rattlesnakes, adders and sidewinders.

How reptiles breed

Reptiles as a group are very quiet, capable only of hisses or hoarse roars, so they rarely make breeding calls. Some male reptiles have courtship 'dances', to show that they are strong and healthy. Male and female mate, and the female lays her leathery-shelled eggs in a suitable place – under stones, in a hollow log, or in soil.

● Some crocodiles make nests of piled-up vegetation for their eggs.

● Female turtles come ashore at night and laboriously dig holes in beach sand, lay their hundred or more eggs, and cover them before retreating back to sea.

● In some lizards and snakes, the babies hatch from the eggs while still inside the mother, and she gives birth to fully formed young.

Tuatara (sphenodon)

The puzzling tuatara

Tuataras live only on a few rocky islands around New Zealand. They look like lizards, but they are rhynchocephalians, a reptile group that was widespread even before the dinosaurs. Tuataras live in burrows by day, and come out at night to eat beetles, spiders and other small animals, and also bird eggs and chicks. Tuataras breed very slowly. Adults do not mate until at least 20 years old, and their eggs do not hatch for 15 months, the longest time for any reptile. Sadly many of the islands where tuataras once survived are now infested with rats, who eat the tuatara eggs. These reptiles are rare and protected.

Baby reptile cuts slit in tough shell with special egg-tooth

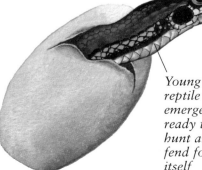

Young reptile emerges ready to hunt and fend for itself

BIRDS

ONLY THREE GROUPS OF ANIMALS can truly fly. They are insects, bats and birds. However, the largest bird, the 2 metre-tall ostrich from Africa, is one of the few kinds of birds that cannot fly at all. The smallest bird, the bee-hummingbird of tropical America, is hardly larger than a bumble-bee. Yet it can fly too fast for us to see, hover and even flit backwards. Birds are vertebrates, with an inner skeleton and backbone, and four limbs. They are warm-blooded, like mammals, and so active even in very cold weather. The unique bird feature is its feathers. They form a light, strong, coloured covering over the body, to keep the bird warm and camouflaged. They also form a large, airtight surface on the wings, for flight. And they can be fanned, twisted and tilted for control in the air, so the bird can soar, swoop, turn and dive with amazing skill.

Groups of birds

There are nearly 9,000 kinds, or species, of birds, in about 28 sub-groups. The largest is the passerines, or songbirds, with 5,200 species, including familiar wrens, sparrows, tits, swallows, larks, warblers, finches and blackbirds. The smallest sub-group has only one species – the flightless ostrich. Other flightless birds include South American rheas, Australian emus, New Zealand kiwis, and 16 kinds of penguins on the coasts and icebergs of southern oceans.

Emu, the world's second-largest bird

Parts of a bird

A typical bird is very lightweight, for better flight. Its bones are thin and hollow, and its toothless beak, or bill, lacks heavy teeth and is made of light-yet-strong horn. All birds have large eyes and excellent sight. They can also hear well but their ear openings on the sides of the head are hidden under the head feathers. A few birds, like woodcocks and kiwis, find food by smell, probing their long, nostril-tipped beaks into soil. A bird's front limbs are wings, and the rear limbs are scaly legs with claw-tipped toes.

Primary feathers give main thrust for forward flight

Secondary feathers form aerofoil surface for main lift

Fluffy down feathers under contour feathers keep in body warmth

Wing coverts

Tail feathers can be spread out and tipped down to slow bird down when landing

Skull

Carina (flange or keel on breast bone) for flight muscle attachment

Humerus (upper arm bone)

Ulna and radius (forearm bones)

Carpals (wrist bones)

Carpometacarpus (hand bones)

Digits (finger bones)

FLIGHT FACTS

- The heaviest flying bird is the kori bustard of Africa, which can weigh almost 20 kg.
- The fastest flying bird is the white-throated spine-tailed swift, which may reach speeds of 160 km/h (100 mph).
- The bird with the longest wings is the wandering albatross, at 3.5 m total span.
- But a prehistoric bird from 10 million years ago, the argentavis condor, had wings more than 7 m across.

Hollow central quill

Microscopic hooks

Bird plumage

Birds such as sparrows and owls have dull feathers with mottled plumage, often in shades of green and brown, for camouflage among trees and bushes. Other birds, especially males at breeding time, have very bright feathers. They include birds of paradise, peacocks, lyrebirds and trogons. The males sing loudly, and shake and fan their feathers, to attract mates. Most birds moult, shedding their old feathers and growing new ones, twice each year.

Bird beaks

The shape of a bird's beak is adapted to the type of food it eats.

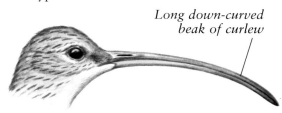

Long down-curved beak of curlew

● Waders such as curlews and avocets have long, thin, needle-like beaks, and probe into seashore sand and mud for worms, small shrimps and shellfish.

Upper mandible of bill

● Parrots and finches have large, strong beaks with powerful jaw muscles and extra leverage, to crack seeds and nuts.

Lower mandible

● Birds of prey, such as eagles, falcons, hawks and owls have sharp, hooked beaks (and also sharp claws called talons) for tearing up victims.

Bird nests and eggs

Most birds breed at a certain time of year, usually in spring or the damp season, when food is more plentiful. Male and female court by singing and displaying their plumage, then mate. The female lays hard-shelled eggs, with developing babies inside. Some bird parents put great effort into making a nest for the eggs. Eagles assemble a huge pile of sticks and twigs, called an eyrie, high on a cliff ledge. Weaverbirds twine leaves, grass and stems together to make a strong, flask-shaped, hollow nest hanging from a tree. But guillemots simply lay their eggs on the bare, rocky ledges of seashore cliffs. Usually, the female sits on or incubates the eggs to keep them warm, while the male fetches her food. Then both parents feed the chicks until they fledge, or learn to fly.

Nest suspended from twig

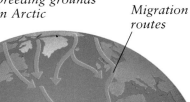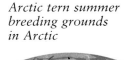

Red-headed weaverbird in its nest

Nest entrance faces downwards

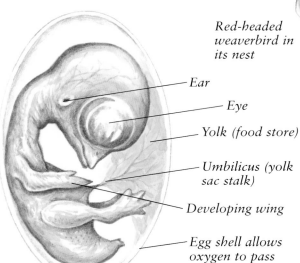

Ear
Eye
Yolk (food store)
Umbilicus (yolk sac stalk)
Developing wing
Egg shell allows oxygen to pass through

Embryo bird inside egg

Spoon-like or spatulate bill shape

● Waterfowl such as ducks, geese and swans have spatula-shaped beaks for dabbling in water and mud.

Treecreeper has upper mandible longer than lower mandible

● Insect-eating birds, like treecreepers and wrens, have slim, tweezer-like beaks for poking into bark and soil.

Bird migrations

Some birds fly long distances each year. They breed in one area, when food and conditions are good, and then leave when conditions become bad, usually for somewhere warmer. These regular to-and-fro journeys are called migrations. The champion migrators are Arctic terns. They breed in the Arctic during the northern summer, then fly around the world to Antarctica for the southern summer. The total yearly round trip may be 30,000 kilometres.

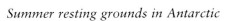

Arctic tern summer breeding grounds in Arctic
Migration routes

Summer resting grounds in Antarctic

MAMMALS 1

MAMMALS ARE PROBABLY the most familiar of all animals. They are generally large, and active in the daytime, like us. They include many pets, farm animals, and also our family, friends and ourselves – since humans are included in the mammal group. A mammal is a warm-blooded vertebrate animal covered with fur or hair, which feeds its babies on milk. The milk is made in the female's milk or mammary glands – the unique feature that gives mammals their name. Mammals vary in size from pygmy shrews, smaller than your thumb, to the biggest animal in the world, the blue whale. The fastest land animal, the cheetah, is a mammal. So is the biggest land animal, the elephant, and the tallest, the giraffe. Mammals live in every habitat on Earth, from bats in the skies, to monkeys in trees, moles underground, seals on seashores, and whales and dolphins in the open ocean. There are three main mammal groups – monotremes, marsupials and placentals (see next page).

European hedgehog has about 5,000 spines

Mammal defences

Plant-eating mammals are prey for meat-eaters. Some have defensive weapons, such as sharp hooves, horns, antlers or tusk-like teeth. Porcupines, which eat roots, fruits, berries and bulbs, have sharp spines called quills, which they rattle to scare the enemy. Hedgehogs also have a spiny covering. The spines are very long, thick, sharp-tipped versions of normal mammal hair or fur. When in danger, the hedgehog tucks in its head and legs and rolls into a ball. Muscles in its skin pull the spines from their laid-back positions into a more upright angle, making it much less tempting as prey. Large mammals such as elephants, rhinos and hippos use their size, bulk and power to overthrow and crush the enemy. The main defences of small mammals like mice and voles are extremely good senses, quick reactions, speed, and small size as they disappear into a little crack or hole. Another form of defence is living in herds (see below right).

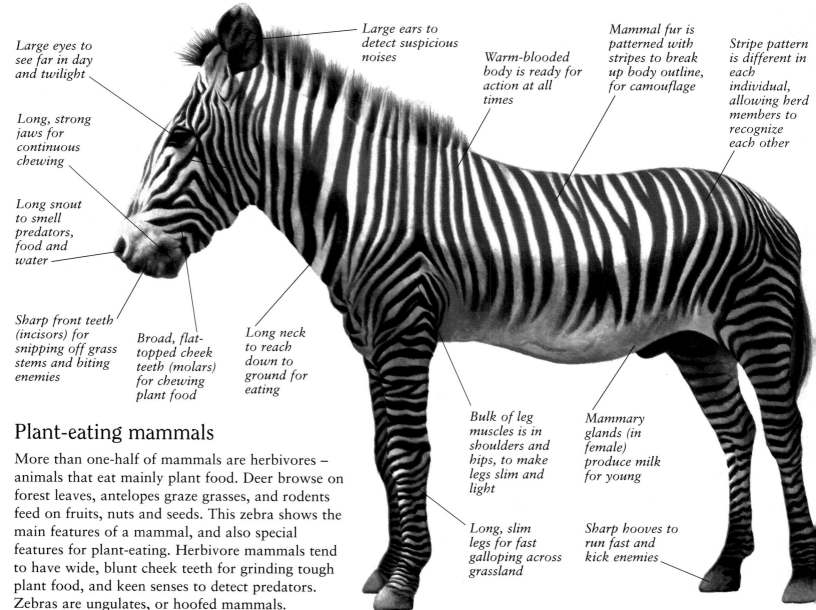

Large eyes to see far in day and twilight

Large ears to detect suspicious noises

Warm-blooded body is ready for action at all times

Mammal fur is patterned with stripes to break up body outline, for camouflage

Stripe pattern is different in each individual, allowing herd members to recognize each other

Long, strong jaws for continuous chewing

Long snout to smell predators, food and water

Sharp front teeth (incisors) for snipping off grass stems and biting enemies

Broad, flat-topped cheek teeth (molars) for chewing plant food

Long neck to reach down to ground for eating

Bulk of leg muscles is in shoulders and hips, to make legs slim and light

Mammary glands (in female) produce milk for young

Long, slim legs for fast galloping across grassland

Sharp hooves to run fast and kick enemies

Plant-eating mammals

More than one-half of mammals are herbivores – animals that eat mainly plant food. Deer browse on forest leaves, antelopes graze grasses, and rodents feed on fruits, nuts and seeds. This zebra shows the main features of a mammal, and also special features for plant-eating. Herbivore mammals tend to have wide, blunt cheek teeth for grinding tough plant food, and keen senses to detect predators. Zebras are ungulates, or hoofed mammals.

Monotremes

A monotreme mammal mother does not give birth to babies, like other mammals. She lays eggs. The babies hatch out and then she feeds them on her milk. There are only three kinds of monotremes: the platypus from Australia, and the short- and long-beaked echidnas (spiny anteaters) from New Guinea and Australia.

Platypus has webbed feet for swimming in creeks and billabongs

Manatee's front limbs are flippers

Long meal-times

Plant food is usually plentiful, but compared to meat, it is tough to chew and difficult to digest. So plant-eating mammals, especially those consuming stringy grasses and woody twigs, spend much more time feeding, compared to meat-eaters. Large herbivores such as elephants, rhinos and sea-cows eat for up to 20 hours daily. The type of sea-cow called the manatee feeds under cover of darkness. It munches water plants in coastal waters for a minute or two and then comes up to the surface to breathe.

Safety in numbers

One form of defence is to live in a large group, such as a herd. Many larger plant-eating mammals, like bison, zebras, wildebeest and Thomson's gazelles (below), do this. At any one time, most members of the herd are feeding or resting. But there are likely to be a few who are alert, watching and listening and sniffing for danger. If trouble is detected, they can warn the others with alarm cries or sudden movements. As the herd rushes to escape, it is difficult for a predator to single out one individual.

Marsupials

There are about 265 species of marsupials, or pouched mammals. They include kangaroos, wallabies, koalas, wombats, bandicoots, possums and opossums, and also fierce hunters such as the native tiger-cat or quoll of Australia. Marsupial babies are born tiny and hairless. They crawl to their mother's pouch (marsupium), where they feed on her milk and continue to grow. Most marsupials live in Australia, with some in South America and a few, such as the Virginia opossum, in North America.

MAIN GROUPS OF MAMMALS

Here are the main groups, or orders, of the mammals known as placental mammals (as explained on the following page). Almost one-half of all mammal species are rodents, and nearly one-quarter are bats.

EVERYDAY NAMES	GROUP NAME	NUMBER OF SPECIES
Cats, dogs, wolves, bears, foxes, weasels, otters, mongooses, hyaenas	Carnivores	230
Whales, dolphins, porpoises	Cetaceans	76
Seals, sea-lions, walrus	Pinnipeds	33
Sea-cows (manatees, dugong)	Sirenians	4
Lemurs, bushbabies, monkeys, apes, humans	Primates	182
Tree-shrews	Scandentians	18
Flying lemurs, colugos	Dermopterans	2
Elephants	Proboscideans	2
Hyraxes	Hyracoideans	11
Aardvark	Tubulidents	1
Horses, zebras, asses, tapirs, rhinos	Perissodactyls	16
Camels, pigs, peccaries, hippos, deer, giraffe, antelopes, gazelles, cattle, sheep, goats	Artiodactyls	187
Squirrels, beavers, gophers, rats, mice, lemmings, gerbils, jerboas, guinea-pigs, chinchillas, porcupines, mole-rats	Rodents	1,702
Rabbits, hares, pikas	Lagomorphs	58
Elephant-shrews	Macroscelideans	15
Moles, desmans, shrews, hedgehogs, tenrecs, solenodons	Insectivores	345
Anteaters, sloths, armadillos	Edentates	29
Pangolins	Philodonts	7
Bats, flying foxes	Chiropterans	950

MAMMALS 2

About one-third of all mammals are mainly carnivorous, or meat-eating. They include the cat family, from tigers to pet cats, as well as the dog family, including wolves, coyotes, jackals and foxes. Other meat-eaters are the generally smaller but very fierce predators known as mustelids – weasels, stoats, polecats, martens, otters, mink, badgers, skunks and similar mammals. The hyaenas and the civets – a group which includes the cat-like civets, genets and linsangs, and the mongooses – are meat-eaters too, and so are raccoons. All of these belong the main mammal group called Carnivora. They are mostly strong and agile, with long, pointed teeth and claws to seize, stab and tear up prey.

Apart from the members of the Carnivora group, many other mammals also eat meat, but in different forms. Dolphins prey on fish and squid. Insectivores, like hedgehogs, moles and shrews, eat meaty but tiny prey, such as insects and worms.

Meat-eating mammals

This lioness shows the main features of a carnivorous or hunting mammal. They include sharp teeth, especially the long, fang-like front teeth called canines, and sharp toe claws. The canines are adapted for grabbing, tearing and ripping prey. The cheek teeth (mainly premolars and molars) of cats and dogs are unlike the broad crushing teeth of herbivorous mammals. They are called carnassial teeth and have strong, sharp ridges. These are used to shear and slice up the food, especially the tough parts of the carcass such as sinews and gristle. In hyaenas, these carnassial teeth are massive. Being close to the joints of the jaws, they have great leverage and can produce huge pressure to crush even bones. Like their prey, carnivorous mammals need keen senses such as sight and hearing. Cats, with their large eyes and long whiskers for feeling the way, tend to be night hunters. Dogs such as wolves hunt mainly by day or at twilight. Bears are also included in the main Carnivora group, but they have a much more varied diet than meat alone (see below right). Strangely, the pandas are also in the Carnivora, because of their general body features and evolutionary links. Yet the giant panda eats almost nothing but bamboo.

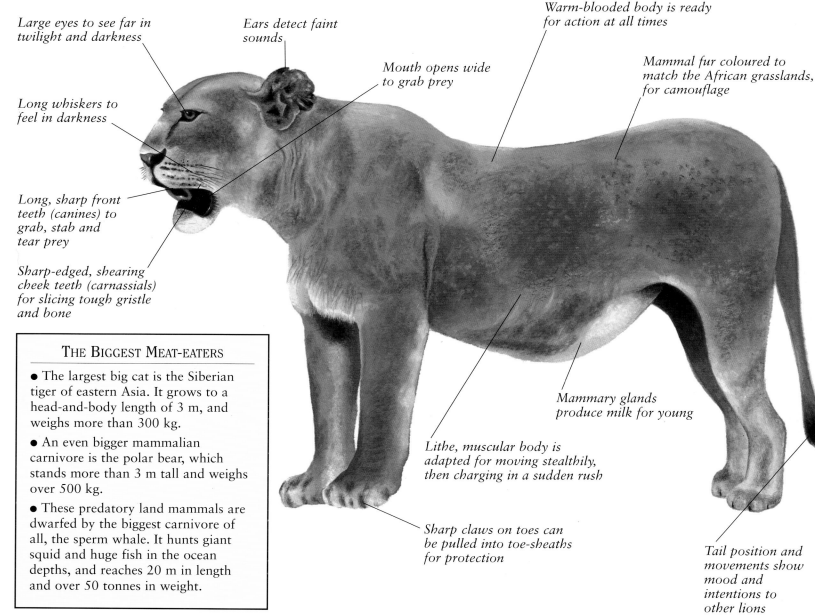

Large eyes to see far in twilight and darkness

Ears detect faint sounds

Mouth opens wide to grab prey

Warm-blooded body is ready for action at all times

Mammal fur coloured to match the African grasslands, for camouflage

Long whiskers to feel in darkness

Long, sharp front teeth (canines) to grab, stab and tear prey

Sharp-edged, shearing cheek teeth (carnassials) for slicing tough gristle and bone

Mammary glands produce milk for young

Lithe, muscular body is adapted for moving stealthily, then charging in a sudden rush

Sharp claws on toes can be pulled into toe-sheaths for protection

Tail position and movements show mood and intentions to other lions

THE BIGGEST MEAT-EATERS

● The largest big cat is the Siberian tiger of eastern Asia. It grows to a head-and-body length of 3 m, and weighs more than 300 kg.

● An even bigger mammalian carnivore is the polar bear, which stands more than 3 m tall and weighs over 500 kg.

● These predatory land mammals are dwarfed by the biggest carnivore of all, the sperm whale. It hunts giant squid and huge fish in the ocean depths, and reaches 20 m in length and over 50 tonnes in weight.

Social mammals

Some mammals live in large groups. They include wolf packs, lion prides, whale schools, monkey troops, and herds of herbivores such as gazelles (shown on the previous pages). In a monkey troop, group members help each other by sharing food, ganging up together against enemies, and grooming each other's fur for lice, fleas and other pests.

Cold body extremities look pinky-blue

Hibernating dormouse

Grooming removes skin pests and also strengthens social links

Hibernation

Some mammals enter a deep sleep, hibernation, during the cold season. This helps to save energy and to make them less noticeable to predators. Their bodies cool down from the usual 35–40°C, to 8°C or less, and all body processes happen very slowly. Dormice, ground squirrels such as the chipmunk and marmot, pikas and many kinds of bats undergo hibernation.

Omnivores

Some mammals eat both meat and plants, depending on what is available. Brown bears eat fish, rabbits and deer, and also feast on roots, fruits and honey. Many monkeys snatch mice, lizards and birds' eggs, but also consume flowers, fruits and berries. These animals are called omnivores, which means they 'eat everything'. Other mammals, such as hyaenas and jackals, and even wolves (below), can be scavengers. They eat dead or dying animals.

Mammal families

In the breeding season, male and female mammals come together to mate. Usually the males display their strength and health by courtship behaviour for the females. Sometimes rival males battle each other, as when male deer rut or male seals fight, to show their strength and win females. Mammal babies develop inside the female's body, in a part called the womb or uterus. In the main subgroup of mammals, the babies receive nourishment through a special body part, the placenta (afterbirth). So this subgroup is called the placental mammals. Usually, the mother feeds and cares for her offspring. In some species, the father helps. Mammals have the longest periods of parental care of any animals. In great apes such as the chimps and gorillas, it lasts for several years.

Flying mammals

A bat's front limbs are large wings, made of very thin, stretchy skin held out by long, thin finger bones. Most bats are small, live in tropical forests and fly only at night, so they are seldom seen by people. They emit very high-pitched squeaks of sound, which bounce off nearby objects. The bat hears the returning echoes and works out what is around, so it can find its way in darkness. (This system, echolocation, is also used by some whales and dolphins.)

Finger bones

Patagium (wing membrane)

Arm bones

PAW-PRINT COLLECTION

You can find out about mammals even when they are not there – by their paw prints. Deer and horses have distinctive hooves. Dog prints are larger than cat prints and have impressions of the claws. Look for paw prints in soft ground such as near a pond. Clean away loose twigs and leaves, press a strip of card in a circle into the soil around the print, and fill it with plaster of paris mixture. Leave it to set. Remove the hard cast and clean it for display in your collection.

ANIMALS AND PEOPLE

EVIDENCE FROM FOSSILS, our own body structure and our genes shows that humans evolved as part of the living world. About two or three million years ago, our very distant ape-like ancestors lived in Africa, hunting animals for meat, and gathering fruits and other plant parts for foods. Our world is now very different. We have clothes, computers, cars and other marvellous inventions. Yet we still rely on animals. We use domesticated species for all kinds of work, such as carrying and pulling. We enjoy the companionship of our tame pets. We appreciate the beauty, sights and sounds of wild creatures such as birds and insects. And billions of people depend on animals for food – whether from the wild or reared on farms.

Farm animals

Farm animals vary around the world. In some regions, cattle are popular. In drier places, goats may be more productive. Pigs and goats are useful because they eat a very wide range of foods, while sheep are fussier, needing mainly grass. In the cold lands of the north, reindeer are reared. Also, people's eating habits and dietary fashions change. If the meat of crocodiles, ostriches, kangaroos, red deer or wild boar becomes popular, it may become worth farming. On a modern farm, these animals are reared not only for their meat, and perhaps their milk. Their fur, hair or feathers can be made into clothes and textiles. Their skins are treated to produce leathers. Their carcasses are processed into products such as glues, oils and waxes. On a modern intensive farm, very little is wasted.

Changing genes

Many kinds of animals and plants have been altered from their wild ancestors by selective breeding. Most animals on today's farms were produced in this way. In recent years it has been possible to change living things much faster, in one generation, by genetic engineering. Using laboratory methods, animals such as sheep can be cloned – copied exactly, so that all individuals have precisely the same genes, like innumerable identical twins. Or the genes from one species can be extracted from the microscopic cells, in the form of the genetic material DNA, and put into the cells of another species. However, the long-term effects of these changes, such as whether these genetically modified organisms will alter further, or breed with wild relatives, are not known.

Arguments about animals

Some people say that modern, intensive farming methods are cruel. For example, 'battery' chickens are kept in tiny cages, with little room, natural light or fresh air. But others say that these methods are useful because they keep food prices low and allow people to buy more varied meals. If all hens roamed freely, the price of poultry produce could soar.

An ostrich farm – ostrich meat can be healthier than many red meats

Learning about life – and death

Millions of people spend billions in money on, and also many happy hours with, their pets. Pet animals can help us to understand about animal needs and the pet's wild relatives. They encourage people to learn about responsibility and caring for others. They can also help us to find out about friendships, and even how to cope with illness and death.

Working animals

Machines such as trucks and tractors do heavy work and haulage in some countries. In other places, animals do this type of work. Llamas, horses, cattle, donkeys and even elephants can be pack animals, carrying heavy loads over rough ground. Horses, oxen, water-buffaloes and elephants are used as draught animals, pulling ploughs, carts and carriages, or dragging logs. Sometimes, animals go where machines cannot. In cold places, dogs or reindeer pull sleds over bumpy snow and jagged ice. In the sandy desert, camels convey loads easily over the soft ground.

ANIMAL USE OR ABUSE?

Are some animals abused and treated cruelly, rather than simply used?

● Rats, mice, rabbits and other animals are bred for research, especially for experiments with new drugs and medicines.

● Without doubt, the animals suffer. Sometimes the suffering is not totally necessary, since the tests may be repeated for checking, or rival companies may be doing them.

● However, without doubt too, people want better medicines and drugs. Tests on cells in test-tubes can help, but cannot yet replace all animal experiments.

● Testing drugs and similar products on animals is still the main way of making sure they are suitable for people. Indeed, it is the law in most countries around the world.

Special uses

Some animals are specially trained to help people. Sniffer dogs smell out illegal substances such as smuggled drugs. Guide dogs are the 'eyes' of people who cannot see properly, and very often, their close companions too. Mounted police patrol on their horses at large events, to aid crowd control. Some people relax and recover their health by stroking specially trained, very docile pet cats and dogs.

FIND OUT ABOUT ANIMAL PRODUCTS

Some people do not eat any type of animal meat or product, including fish, eggs or cheese. Others do not eat meat, but may eat dairy products such as cheese. Still others eat any kind of meat. Such decisions are made for a variety of reasons, including our personal taste, consuming a healthy diet, concerns about animal welfare and the environment, and worries about the way animal products are treated and processed in factories. Look at some animal products, medicines and cosmetics in a local store. What type of information is given on the labelling? Does it have words such as 'organic', 'free-range' and 'cruelty-free'? Are these terms used in the same way by different manufacturers?

LIVING WORLD IN PERIL

WHEN A SPECIES OF LIVING THING dies out, and there are no more left in the world, this is called extinction. It is a natural part of the process of life, death and evolution. Over millions of years, new species have appeared, as others have become extinct. From the evidence of fossils, experts guess that of all the species which have ever existed on Earth, probably more than 95 out of every 100 are now extinct. An average species lasts 5–10 million years, and for much of the history of our planet, a species has become extinct about every 10 years. Extinction still occurs today. But now, it probably happens not at the rate of one species every 10 years, but one species every day. Some estimates are higher, with five species or more disappearing each day. Many of these lost species are small insects and flowers, which science has not even discovered yet, deep in tropical forests. Extinction has speeded up so much because of human activities in the past few hundred years. Various problems facing the living world, and possible answers, are described here.

Hunting and poaching

Some animals are threatened directly by hunting and poaching. They are usually large and powerful species, such as tigers, rhinos, bears, deer, birds of prey, sharks and other big fish. They are shot, poisoned or trapped for various reasons, such as to show the 'bravery' of the hunter and for trophies to sell. They may also be hunted by people who are protecting themselves and their farm animals against attack.

Before the bulldozers

An area of moist tropical forest is home to an enormously complex web of life. It contains at least one hundred times, and perhaps one thousand times, more species than the same area of temperate forest (such as an oak or beech wood). The range of living species in a habitat is known as biodiversity.

Habitat destruction

This is by far the greatest threat to wildlife. People alter natural places for their own use, changing them into farms, factories, mines, roads, houses, schools and other structures. The problem is especially serious in some tropical regions, where the human population is increasing fast, but there are also some of the rarest and most precious wildlife habitats, such as tropical forests, swampy wetlands and coastal coral reefs. The problem of habitat destruction is so serious because it affects not just one or two species, but all species that live in the area. Worldwide changes such as loss of the protective ozone layer in the atmosphere, and the increased greenhouse effect leading to global warming, are also upsetting the delicate balance of nature.

After the bulldozers

The land may be planted with crops, but these usually grow for only a few years, until the nutrients in the thin soil are exhausted. Or it may be turned into roads, which encourage more people and development in the area.

Collecting

Hundreds of species are rare because they are already naturally rare! They are gathered or collected from the wild for people who wish to own and keep rare and exotic species. Of course, this makes them even more scarce. Such

species include cacti and other flowers, colourful birds like parrots, venomous snakes and spiders, and unusual pets like monkeys and apes. Captive breeding of species such as tropical aquarium fish helps to avoid collecting from the wild.

World wildlife laws

International laws help to protect rare species, such as tigers, trees, snails and wildflowers. CITES, the Convention on International Trade in Endangered Species, forbids people to buy, sell or trade protected species, or products from them such as their tusks, flowers, furs or bones, unless they are properly licensed to do so.

Eco-tourism

The idea of eco-tourism is that people pay money to experience rare species in the wild – visit gorillas in their mountain home, stroke whales at sea, or feed sharks on a coral reef. The tourism is carefully controlled so that it affects the wildlife as little as possible, and the money funds more wildlife conservation projects.

THE 'RED LISTS'

- The IUCN, International Union for the Conservation of Nature, publishes regularly updated 'Red Data Lists' of animals and plants which are threatened in some way.
- The latest list of animals has more than 5,200 species, including 231 types of bats, 733 fish (one species being the great white shark) – and 806 kinds of snails!

Pollution

Vast areas are polluted by unnatural, artificial chemicals. Acid rain damages trees and soil, gets into streams and ponds, and harms fish and other water creatures. Chemicals from industry and our own rubbish and refuse soak into the soil or poison waterways. Intensive farming also pollutes land and water, with pesticides and concentrated fertilizers.

Birds killed by oil pollution

Setting up sanctuaries

National parks, wildlife reserves and nature sanctuaries conserve some wild places. People may be allowed into certain areas, to enjoy the scenery, plants and animals, while other areas are fully protected. Such areas range from a small wood or pond to a vast area of land or sea, the size of a country. In 1994 the Southern Ocean around Antarctica was declared a huge sanctuary where the hunting of great whales and other threatened animals is now forbidden. But sanctuaries must usually be large. A single tiger needs 50 sq km or more of forest to hunt in. And several dozen tigers are needed for a sustainable population that avoids the problems of inter-breeding among close relatives. So a small tiger reserve of a few hectares is less useful for the long term.

GONE FOR EVER

- **1665** The dodo, a turkey-sized flightless bird from the Indian Ocean island of Mauritius.
- **About 1770** Steller's sea-cow, a huge but peaceful plant-eater of the North Pacific Arctic region, 9 m long and weighing 6 tonnes.
- **1914** The passenger pigeon of North America, once so common that its flocks numbered millions.
- **1936** The thylacine (Tasmanian wolf or tiger), a dog-like marsupial suspected of attacking sheep.
- **1952** The Bali tiger, the smallest variety of the tiger species.

INDEX

A
acid rain 37
algae 10, 11
alligators 26, 27
amphibians 16, 17, 22, 24-25
anemones 17, 18
animals 8, 13, 16-17
    and people 34-35
    and plants 14
annelid worms 17, 19
ants 20
antelopes 30, 31
apes 31, 34, 37
arachnids 20, 21
Archaeopteryx 9
arthropods 17, 20-21
asexual reproduction 19
axolotl 25

B
backbone 22, 26, 28
bacteria 9
barnacles 16, 20
bats 28, 30, 31, 33, 37
    pollination 13
beaks 28, 29
bears 31, 32, 33
    threatened 36
beetles 20, 21
birds 8, 17, 28-29, 36
    evolution 26
    threatened species 37
blue-green algae 9
bones 23, 24, 28
    fossils 17

C
cacti 10, 15, 37
caecilians 25
camels 16, 31, 35
camouflage
    birds 28, 29
    fish 23
    mammals 30, 32
    reptiles 26
carbon dioxide 12, 22
carnivores 31, 32-33
cartilaginous fish 23
cats 31, 32, 33
cattle 31, 34 , 35
cells 8, 9, 12, 16, 18
    genetic engineering 34
centipedes 17, 20-21
chlorophyll 10, 12

chordates 17
clubmosses 11
coal 15
cockroaches 20-21
conifer trees 11, 14
conservation 37
copepods 20
corals 17, 18, 19
crabs 17, 20-21
crocodiles 26, 27
crustaceans 17, 20

D
deer 30, 31, 33, 36
dinosaurs 11, 16, 17, 26
diseases 8, 9, 15, 19
DNA 9, 34
dogs 31, 32, 33, 35
dolphins 30, 31, 32, 33
domestic animals 34-35

E
earthworms 17, 19
echinoderms 17, 18-19
eco-tourism 37
edelweiss 10
eels 23
eggs
    amphibians' 24
    birds' 29
    fish 23
    mammals' 31
    reptiles' 26, 27
    snails' 19
elephants 30, 31, 35
embryos 13, 23, 24, 29
emus 28
evolution 9, 11, 16, 22, 34, 36
exoskeleton 20
extinction 16, 36-37

F
farming 8, 14, 37
    animals 16, 30, 34
feathers 28, 29, 34
ferns 10, 11
fertilization 12, 19, 23, 24
finches 28, 29
fins 22, 23
fish 16, 17, 22-23, 37
flatfish 23
flatworms 17, 19
flowering plants 8, 10-11, 12-13
    extinction 36, 37

fossils 9, 11, 16, 34, 36
    fuels 15
foxes 31, 32
frogs 24-25
fruits 11, 13, 14
fungus 8, 9, 11
fur 30, 32, 34

G
gazelles 31, 33
genetics 9, 34
germination 13, 14
germs 8
giant panda 32
gills 22, 24
giraffe 30, 31
global warming 36
goats 31, 34
grass 8, 10, 11, 34
greenhouse effect 36
growth 8, 16
gulper eels 16

H
habitats 10, 16, 26, 30
    destruction 36
hair 30, 34
hedgehogs 30, 31, 32
herbivorous mammals 30-31
herbs 10, 11, 14
herds 30, 31, 33
hibernation 33
hippos 30, 31
hooves 30, 33
horns 17, 30
horsehair worms 19
horses 31, 33, 35
horsetail plants 11
humans 30, 31, 34
hummingbirds 13, 28
hyenas 32, 33

I
iguanas 26
insectivorous mammals 32
insects 8, 16, 17, 20-21, 24
    extinction 36
    flight 28
invertebrates 18-19

J
jellyfish 16, 17, 18-19

K

kangaroos 31
kiwis 28

L

lateral line 22
leaves 11, 12-13, 14
leeches 19
lichens 11
lions 32, 33
liver flukes 19
liverworts 10-11
living things 8-9
    extinction 36
lizards 26, 27

M

mammals 16, 17, 28, 30-31, 32-33
    evolution 26
marsupials 30, 31, 37
medicines 15, 35
metamorphosis 24
migration 29
milk 30, 31, 32, 34
millipedes 16, 17, 20-21
moles 30, 32
molluscs 17, 19, 21
moneran kingdom 8, 9
monkeys 30, 31, 33
    threatened species 37
monotremes 30, 31
mosses 10-11
mushrooms 8, 9
mussels 8, 16, 21
mustelids 32

N

nematode worms 17, 19
newts 24-25
nudibranchs 21
nutrients 10, 12, 14, 19
nuts 13, 14

O

octopus 17, 21
omnivorous mammals 33
oxygen 12, 22, 29
oysters 8, 21

P

parasites 8, 19, 21
parrots 29, 37
passerine birds 28
penguins 28

people 14-15, 34-35
pests 8, 15
pets 8, 16, 30, 34, 35
    threatened species 37
photosynthesis 12
phyla 17, 18, 19, 20
pigs 31, 34
placental mammals 30, 31
plants 8, 10-11, 12-13
    as food 14-15, 30-31
platyhelminthes 17
platypus 31
pollination 12-13
pollution 8, 11, 37
predators 18, 24, 30, 32
primates 31
protist kingdom 8, 9

R

rabbits 31, 35
recycling 9, 19
reindeer 34, 35
reproduction 8, 16, 19
    amphibians 24, 25
    birds 29
    fish 23
    plants 12
    reptiles 27
reptiles 16, 17, 26-27
rhinos 30, 31, 36
rodents 30, 31
roots 12, 13, 14
roundworms 17, 19

S

salamanders 24-25
scorpions 21
sea-cows 31, 37
sea-lilies 16
sea urchins 17, 18-19
seals 30, 31
seaweeds 10-11
seeds 11, 12, 13, 14
senses 16, 22, 30, 32
sharks 16, 22, 23, 36, 37
sheep 31, 34
shellfish 16, 17, 18
shrews 30, 31, 32
skeletons 23, 24, 26, 28
slugs 21
snails 17, 19, 21, 37
snakes 26, 27
songbirds 28
sowbugs 20

sparrows 28, 29
spiders 8, 17, 20-21, 37
sponges 16, 17, 18, 19
springtails 20, 21
squid 17, 21
starfish 16, 17, 18-19
stick-insects 20, 21
symbiosis 11

T

tadpoles 24-25
tapeworms 19
teeth 17, 23, 30, 32
terrapins 26, 27
tigers 32, 36, 37
toads 24-25
toadstools 9
tortoises 26, 27
tree frogs 25
trees 8, 10, 11
trilobites 16
tuataras 27
turtles 26, 27

U

ungulate mammals 30

V

vertebrates 17
    amphibians 24
    birds 28
    fish 22
    mammals 30
    reptiles 26
viruses 9

W

warm-blooded animals 28, 30, 32
water-bears 17
whales 17, 30, 31, 32, 33, 37
wings 20, 28, 29, 33
wolves 31, 32, 33
wood 11, 14, 15
wood lice 20
worm-lizards 26, 27
worms 16, 17, 19
wrens 28, 29

Y

yeasts 9

Z

zebras 30, 31

ACKNOWLEDGEMENTS

The publishers wish to thank the following artists who have contributed to this book:

David Ashby, Mike Atkinson, Andy Beckett, Martin Camm, Wayne Ford, Chris Forsey, Roger Kent, Kuo Kang Chen, Stuart Lafford, Alan Male, Julie Pickering, Gillian Platt, Terry Riley, Martin Salisbury, Guy Smith, Sue Stitt.

The publishers wish to thank the following for supplying photographs for this book:

Page 9 (B/R) Corbis; 19 (C) G.I.Bernard/Oxford Scientific Films; 25 (T/L) R.L.Manuel/Oxford Scientific Films; 34 (T/R) Remi Benali-Stephen Ferry-Life Magazine/Gamma-Liaison/Frank Spooner Pictures; 35 (C/R) Didier Lebrun/Photo News/Gamma/Frank Spooner Pictures; 37 (T) E.T.Archive.

All other photographs from Miles Kelly archives.